Look at YOU, Piper Lou!

Written & Illustrated by Jillian DuBois

Look at YOU, Piper Lou!

Copyright © by Jillian DuBois

First Edition 2021

All rights reserved.

No part of this publication may be reproduced in any form, or by any means, electronic or mechanical, including photocopying, recording, or any information browsing, storage, or retrieval system, without permission from the publisher.

Imparted Joy LLC

Dedicated with gratitude to all of the selfless humans who unconditionally adore furry friends and give happy homes to those who need hope and compassion.

Piper Lou gives special thanks to Dr. Don Woodman & staff at Animal Hospital of Northwood in Clearwater, FL (animalhospitalofnorthwood.com) for the excellent care given to ALL animals who require careful attention.

And to the volunteer pals at Labrador Retriever Rescue of Florida (lrrof.org) who serve generously with heart & never-ending love.

Generous appreciation to my editorial team: Traci Nicole Smith & Livia Chan. You amaze me with your unwavering devotion and friendship.

Thank you to Blake from #RoadToAwesome for making a surprise appearance!

The sparkling sun was calmly peeking through the trees one late spring afternoon.

The warm air was silent inside the weathered doghouse where the young pup lived.

Suddenly startled, she cautiously poked her head out as she looked toward the empty house.

Her owners were gone for what seemed like days. They left her alone before, but this time, it felt strangely different.

Deciding to leave her little domain, she chose a direction and bravely began to walk alone.

She was unsure of where to go, but she knew the journey would lead her somewhere.

Helpful hands and happy faces passed by as she eagerly wagged her tail for attention.

Generous handouts of delicious treats were offered. Thoughtful pup friends shared barks of kindness.

A comforting pat on the head from caring bystanders gave her hopeful dreams of a forever family.

Sympathetic pals provided comfy places where she could stay safe and sleep peacefully.

She whimpered softly to nearby friends on her journey in hopes they could calm her anxious heart.

There were smiles from strangers everywhere she turned. Big, small, short, and tall. But no one took her home.

Without warning, she was quickly picked up by a big truck that smelled of sweet flowers.

"It's alright, little one, everything will be fine," the driver tenderly whispered.

But everything was not fine. She was reluctant to let her guard down.

The kind driver delivered her to a local animal shelter where she immediately felt fearful.

Later that night, she could not sleep.
She had visions of running and
romping around happily.

Little did she know, there was someone special wishing for a pup JUST like her.

The next morning, Charli's family drove to the shelter. They excitedly talked about the possibility of a new pet.

"Today will be the best day ever!"
Charli exclaimed with anticipation.

Charli skipped through the door and looked around. She ran right up to a kennel and asked, "I pick this one. Can we adopt HER, Daddy, please?"

They brought her home and named her Piper Lou. New friends came to celebrate her arrival.

There were endless belly rubs, balls to chase, soft beds, savory snacks, and more hugs than ever.

Piper Lou found true love and loyalty. She inhaled deeply and exhaled pure joy to everyone around her.

Charli and Piper Lou became the best of buddies as they snuggled and cuddled together.

Charli told her many stories and secrets of life as they took long walks.

Piper Lou listened with undivided attention.

Piper Lou was content and understood that this was exactly what genuine acceptance felt like.

When you patiently stop and look around,
you will find that life has its ups and downs.

Choose to dream and to listen to your heart with confidence. Through the hard times, there will always be hope.

You are loved.
You are valued.
You are enough.
Look at YOU, Piper Lou!

coconut

dexter

ray + buc

phoenix

jojo

gizmo

bowie

mason

Piper Lou's Crew

Thank you to our friends!

cali

jack

GG

sterling

ressie

truman

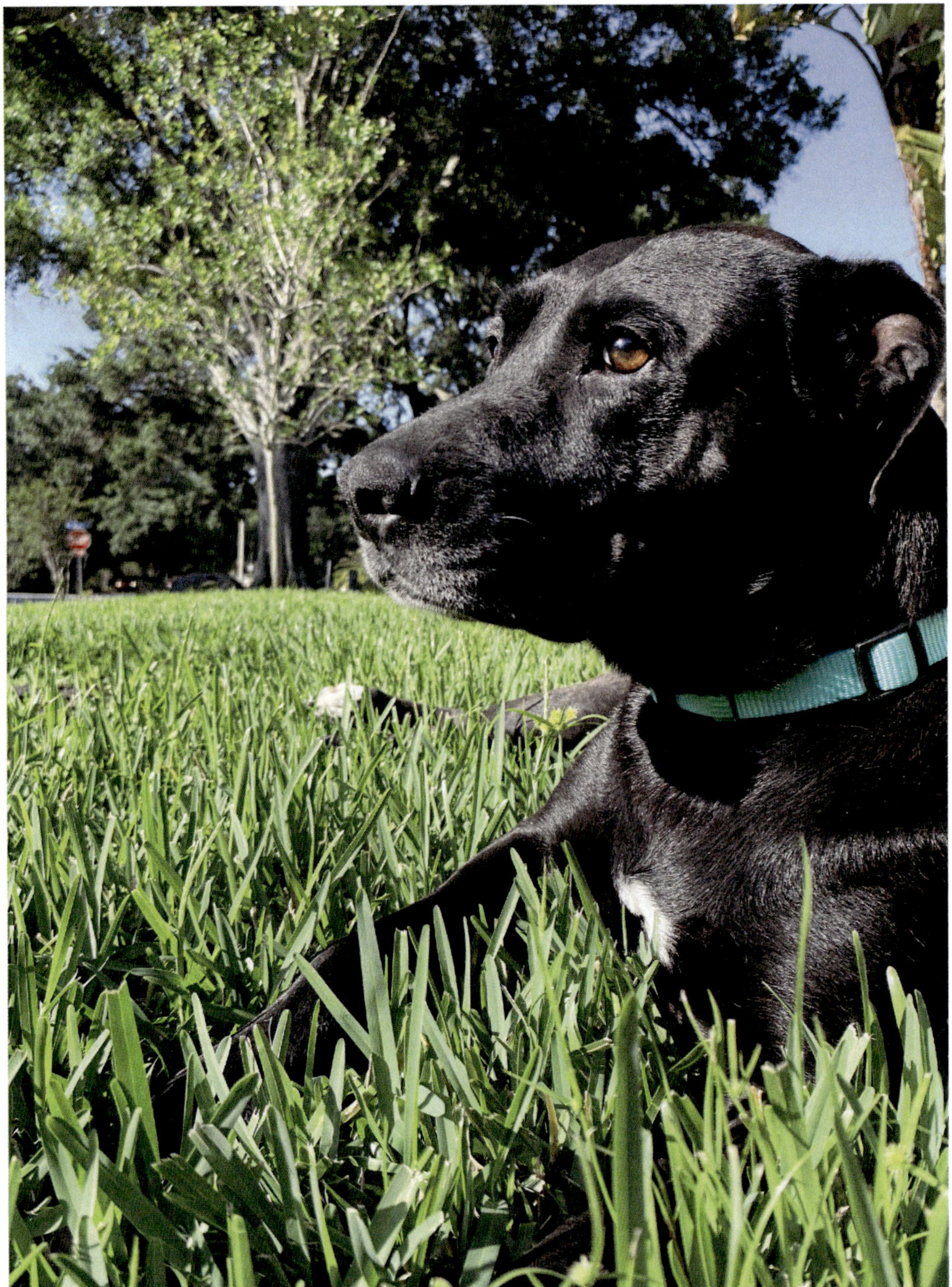

To the readers,

Piper Lou's story is very special to my heart.
She's our pup that we took in and adopted as our own.
From the moment we brought her home, we KNEW she sensed this was her forever family. She fully enjoys chasing squirrels, playing frisbee, and going for long car rides. She is a bed hog, snores, and will not let anyone out of her sight for long.
There is something incredibly loyal about the love of a pet that is accepting of true love. I have a feeling that there are people out there who need the same empathy and kindheartedness.
I hope you find this story to be one that inspires YOU to acknowledge that life is precious and how we need others around us to share in our hopes and dreams.

YOU are enough. You are loved, worthy, and capable to be all that you dream to be. Focus on all that brings you joy.

Love, Jillian and Piper Lou

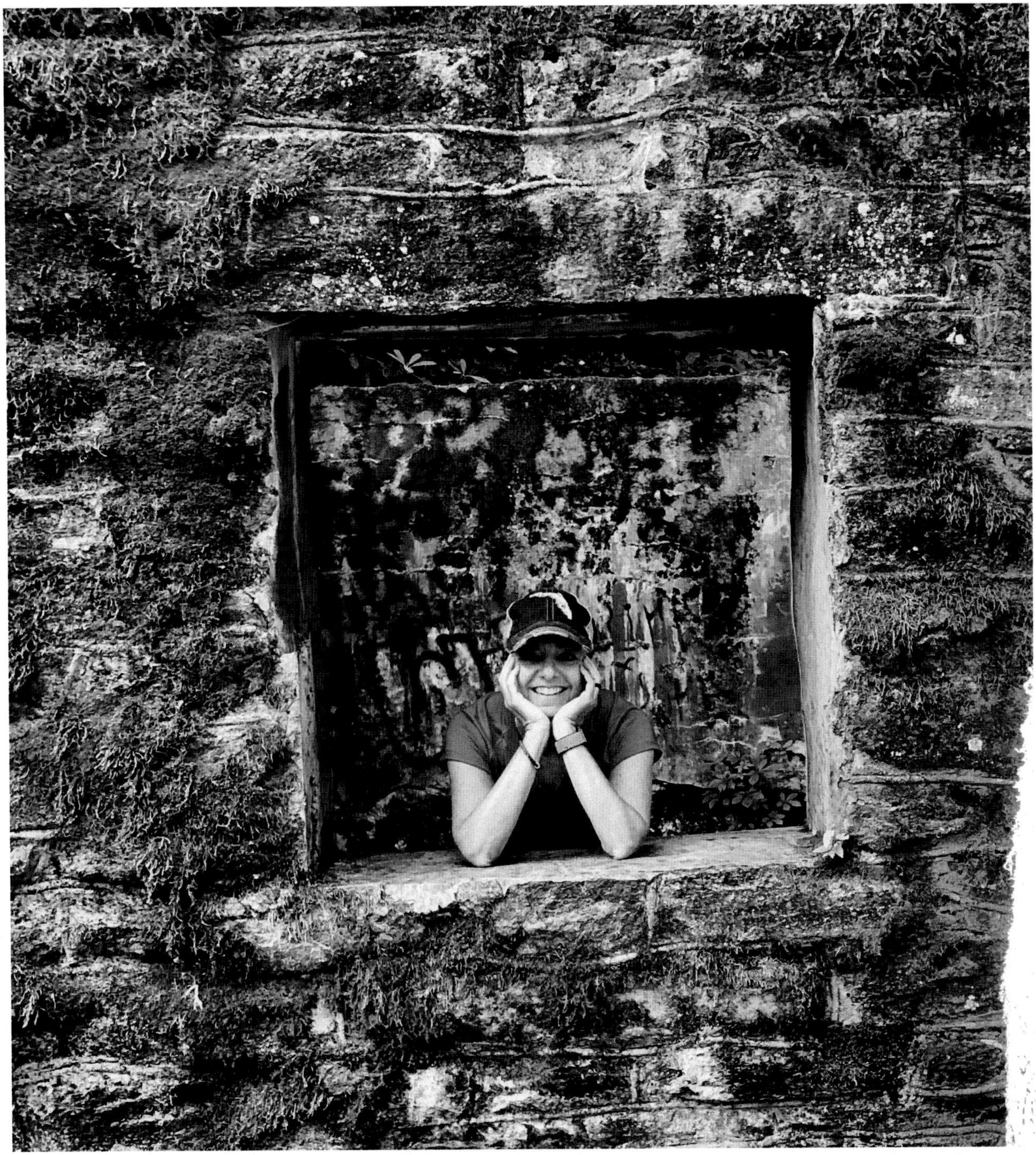

Jillian's journey continues to bring joy and fulfillment as she thrives on building authentic relationships with her students in the classroom and guiding them through curiosity and wonder.

She uses her voice to foster hope for equity and empathy. Her passion is to initiate, instill, and infuse joy to those in education by focusing her efforts on listening and stretching alongside colleagues and friends.

Jillian personally spends her free time outdoors, soaking up the sun and surf on local Florida beaches, and finding new paths to hike with her husband, son, and Piper Lou.

This is Jillian's third published book as an author and illustrator. Connect with her through www.impartedjoy.com or on Twitter @JillDuBois22 to say hello!

www.impartedjoy.com

Made in the USA
Columbia, SC
23 June 2023